THE VIETNAM BROWN WATER NAVY

RIVERINE AND COASTAL WARFARE 1965-69

Text by Gordon L. Rottman
Color plates by Hubert Cance

CONCORD
PUBLICATIONS COMPANY

We welcome authors who can help
expand our range of books. If you
would like to submit material,
please feel free to contract us.

We are always on the look-out for new,
unpublished photos for this series.
If you have photos or slides or
information you feel may be useful to
future volumes, please send them to us
for possible future publication.
Full photo credits will be given upon
publication.

ISBN 962-361-617-1

printed in Hong Kong

The Mekong Delta is the world's largest river delta. This photograph represents but a small part of the Delta, but demonstrates the difficulties in navigating its endless waterways and locating an elusive enemy intimately familiar with his environment. All the light areas are water and much of the "ground" under the trees and dense brush was inundated or deep mud. A patrol boat on the river would appear no larger than a pinhead. A sampan would be but a pinpoint. (Leroy Wilson)

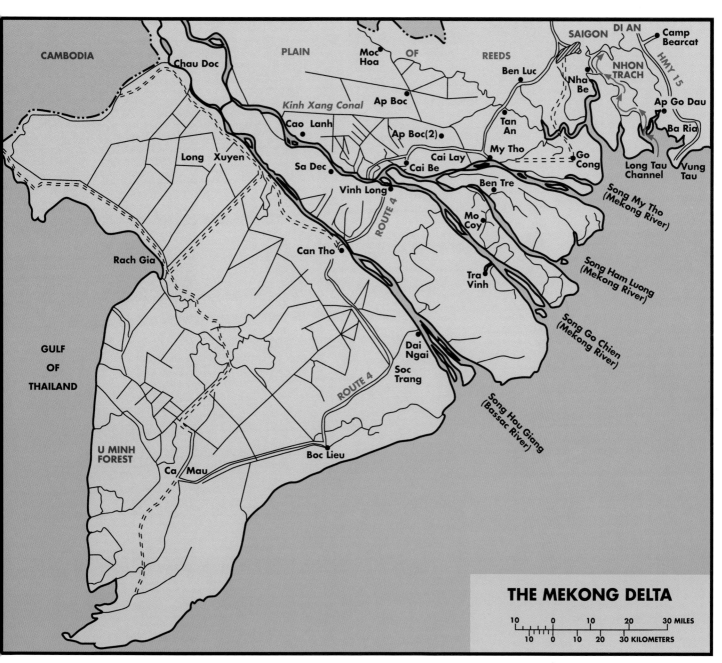

THE MEKONG DELTA

INTRODUCTION

Riverine and coastal warfare were not new to Vietnam when the United States Navy entered the war in the mid-1960s. They had long been practiced by the modern French and Vietnamese navies as well as by the ancient Vietnamese, Chinese, and Khamers since the earliest days of warfare in the aquatic world of the vast expanse of the Mekong Delta.

The vast Mekong Delta contains the world's most extensive navigational and drainage canal system. Begun in 800 AD and continued by subsequent generations and the industrious French, it contains some 2,400km of navigable natural waterways and 4,000km of manmade channels of varying width and depth. However, over half of these had deteriorated to the point where they were navigable only at high tide. The Viet Cong (VC) had obstructed some canals and others were choked with fish traps. The Delta was dominated by the mighty Song Mekong (Song- River), the world's eleventh longest, flowing 2,600 miles (4,200km) out of the mountains of Tibet, forming the borders between Burma and Laos and Thailand and Laos, through Cambodia and Vietnam and into the South China Sea. Inside Cambodia the Mekong branches off into the Song Hou Giang (Bassac River), which parallels it to the south. Some 50 miles (80km) from the coast the Mekong splits into three main rivers (from north to south): Song My Tho, Song Ham Luong, and Song Co Chien. A separate river, the Nhon Trach, delineating the eastern edge of the Delta, flows from the north through the Rung Sat. The Rung Sat (Forest of Assassins) is a dense mangrove swamp and river estuary containing a labyrinth of winding rivers and channels.

The Delta encompasses 10,190 square miles (40,000km^2), constituting a quarter of South Vietnam's land area. One-third of the Delta is marsh, wooded swamps, and forests. The largest of these is the U Minh Forest on the Delta's west coast. The Delta's northern portion is covered by the treeless Plain of Reeds, inundated up to 10 ft. (3m) in the wet season. Waterways are edged with near continuous lines of dense vegetation providing excellent positions from which to ambush river traffic. The rest of the Delta is covered with rice paddies making it the world's most productive rice growing region. Other regional industries include fishing and cement production in the Seven Mountains, an area of low forested, rocky hills in the northwest.

The effects of tides in the Delta region, even far inland, are difficult to predict due to the complex nature of the interconnected waterways. Twice daily the tidal flow influences the current speed and even changes the direction of flow. Tidal fluctuations vary up to 13 ft. (4m).

An estimated eight-million of Vietnam's 20-million population inhabited the Delta. The road network was extremely limited and what roads there were had to cross countless canals and waterways, over which the VC had destroyed most of the bridges. The Delta's real roads are its waterways with sampans the main mode of transportation. Even villages were either floating, built on stilts, or with individual homes on earth mounds.

Malaria and dengue fever is rampant year around as are leeches, poisonous snakes, and vicious ants. The water is unfit to drink. During the dry season, December to March, salt water intrudes 20-50 miles inland up the waterways. The April to November wet, or monsoon season, brings over 80 inches of rain. Temperatures are in the 80-100°F (26-38°C) range with equally high humidity. Soldiers on foot in the Delta were exhausted after three days in the field and required at least two days to recover from constantly wet feet. Longer duration operations led to immersion foot, rashes, and skin ulcers.

While most of the Mekong Delta was encompassed within the IV Corps Tactical Zone (CTZ), its extreme northeast portion lay within III CTZ. This included the infamous Rung Sat Special Zone, long a VC stronghold, through which the Long Tau Channel runs from Vung Tau on the coast to Vietnam's main seaport and capital, Saigon, 30 miles (48km) from the sea.

In mid-1966, the VC in the Delta numbered about 20,000 Main Force troops and 50,000 Local Force part-time guerrillas backed by 11,000 political cadre and infrastructure, the shadow government of the National Liberation Front. They were organized into three regiments, 20 independent battalions, 69 independent companies, and 11 platoons. They received logistical support from North Vietnamese Army (NVA) bases in Cambodia to the north, sympathetic civilians, and material captured from the Army of the Republic of Vietnam (ARVN).

ARVN presence in IV CTZ numbered some 40,000 troops. In the north was the marginal quality 7th Division at My Tho. The extremely poor quality 9th Division was in the central area at Sa Dec and the very good 21st Division, at Bac Lieu, was responsible for the south. Additionally, there were five ranger battalions and three company-size armored cavalry squadrons. There were dozens of paramilitary Regional Force companies and Popular Force platoons (Ruff-Puffs), which secured towns and villages. There were also 16 US Special Forces-advised, battalion-size Civilian Irregular Defense Group (CIDG) camp strike forces. These remote camps were located mainly on the Cambodian border and in the north-central portion of the Delta. Vietnamese Navy (VNN) forces were under the control of the 4th Naval Zone and included River Assault Groups 21-26 and Coastal Groups 34-38 and 41-47 (the Junk Fleet). The 3d, 4th, and 5th Vietnamese Marine Battalions frequently operated in the Delta and were supported by both VNN river assault groups and US Navy river assault divisions.

Prior to the end of 1966, there were no US combat units in IV CTZ. There were, however, advisors; almost 700 officers and 2,000 enlisted men. Army advisors were assigned to ARVN IV CTZ Headquarters and Logistics Command, 16 sector (province) headquarters, and the three ARVN divisions and their regiments. US Navy Advisory Group, Vietnam (NAGV) provided advisors to the VNN's river assault and coastal groups, naval headquarters, and training centers. There were also a small number of US Air Force advisors. One of the most overworked units in Vietnam was the Army's 13th Aviation Battalion (Combat), which was activated in September 1964 from the Delta Aviation Battalion, itself serving since June 1963. It provided helicopter air assault support to the ARVN divisions.

In mid-1966, the situation in the Delta had severely deteriorated. About one-third of VC actions in Vietnam took place in IV CTZ and they controlled about a quarter of the Delta's population. The decision to commit a US riverine force to the Delta was made in late 1965.

The unit selected to provide this unique force was the 9th Infantry Division, reactivated at Ft. Riley, Kansas in February 1966. The Division's 2d Brigade was designated as the Army component of the Mobile Riverine Force. The rest of the Division would conduct normal ground operations. The concept was jointly developed by the Army and Navy with the Nav modifying landing craft and organizing river assau squadrons. Training was conducted through th remainder of 1966 and riverine doctrine further jointl developed. The US Navy had last participated in riverin warfare during the Civil War. Elements of the Divisio began to arrive in Vietnam in December 1966 with the 2 Brigade arriving at the end of February 1967. The Division was based at Bearcat near the Rung Sat Speci Zone. It was comprised of the 2d and 4th Battalions, 47t Infantry; 3d Battalion, 60th Infantry; and the 105m howitzer-armed 3d Battalion, 34th Artillery.

The Navy component was Task Force 117 (Rive Assault Flotilla One) with River Assault Squadron (RAS) 9 and 11. These were to be organized into Mobil Riverine Group ALPHA when RASs 13 and 15 arrived i June 1968 to form Mobile Riverine Group BRAVO ALPHA normally operated in the eastern Delta an BRAVO in west.

The 400-man RASs were subdivided into two rive assault divisions (RAD), each with one or two comman and communications boats, two or three monitors, 1 armored troop carriers, eight assault support patrol boat and a refueler. Attachments included Underwate Demolition Team (UDT) squads, an explosive ordnanc disposal detachment, and a riverine survey team. Th separate RAD 121 was raised for Dong Tam base defens duties.

Dong Tam was built by Army engineers and Nava Mobile Construction Battalions (Seabees) and served a both the headquarters for the Task Force 117 and the 2 Brigade. The base was located 3 miles (5km) west of th town of My Tho on the north bank of the Song My Tho The units themselves rotated between Dong Tam and th afloat Mobile Riverine Base (MRB), which was relocate on Delta rivers as required to support riverine operation The MRB was operated by River Support Squadron (RIVSUPRON 7) comprised of:

2	Barracks Ship, Self-propelled (APB (converted LST)
1	Barracks Ship, Non-self-propelled (APL)
1	Landing Craft Repair Ship (converted LST) (ARL)
1	Landing Ship, Tank (LST)
1	Repair, Berthing, and Messing Barge (YRBM)
2	Harbor Tug, Large (YTB)
1	Net-laying Ship (AN)

After many successful joint operations throughou the Delta, the Mobile Riverine Force began to dissolve i the summer of 1969 as US forces started to withdra from Vietnam. The 2d Brigade, 9th Infantry Divisio departed in July. Task Force 117 (River Assault Flotill One) ceased operations in June was decommissioned i

August with its 184 craft turned over to either the VNN or Task Force 194 (SEALORDS).

Besides the Mobile Riverine Force, the US Navy conducted a number of other operations in Vietnamese inland and inshore waters.

Task Force 115 (Operation MARKET TIME) was the Coastal Surveillance Force. North Vietnam committed major resources and much effort to infiltrate munitions and supplies into South Vietnam by sea. One-hundred-ton trawlers of the North Vietnamese Naval Transportation Group 125 were employed along with hundreds of seagoing junks. The major difficulty facing US Navy and VNN coastal patrol forces was to sift infiltrating craft from the hundreds of legal cargo junks and fishing boats. When formed in early 1965, the Force was initially placed directly under Task Force 71, the Seventh Fleet's Vietnam Patrol Force. Task Force 115 was established in July to operate the Force. Its Patrol Craft, Inshore (PCF) (before 14 August 1968, Patrol Craft, Coastal (Fast) with same classification code) or "Swift boats", were assigned to Boat Squadron 1 with Boat Divisions 101-105. In January 1967, it was redesignated Coastal Squadron 1 and now with Coastal Divisions 11-16. Each division had about 16 PCFs. These were supplemented by Coast Guard Squadron 1, which arrived when Task Force 115 was activated. It was divided into Coast Guard Divisions 11-13, each with eight or nine WPB all-weather patrol boats (cutters). Coastal Squadron 3, with three Patrol Gun Boats (PG) and two Patrol Gun Boats, Hydrofoil (HPG), was commissioned in May 1967. Coastal Squadrons 1 and 3 were placed under Coastal Flotilla One. A total of 144 patrol boats and other craft were assigned to Task Force 115. The Task Force was also responsible for harbor defense under Operation STABLE DOOR. This mission was accomplished by Inshore Underwater Warfare Units (IUWU) 1-5 with a total of 16 Landing Crafts, Personnel, Large (LCPL) (actually patrol boats), 25 Boston Whalers, and eight 45-ft. picket boats.

Task Force 115 intercepted and inspected an average of 16,000 junks and other craft per month. Prior to 1966, the enemy received approximately three-quarters of his supplies by sea. By the end of 1966 it was estimated to have dropped to one-tenth. Most of Task Force 115's craft were turned over to the VNN in 1969-70.

One of the better known operations was Task Force 116 (Operation GAME WARDEN), the River Patrol Force. The Navy was authorized to conduct river warfare operations in the Delta in August 1965 and Task Force 116 was activated in December with River Patrol Squadron 5. The Task Force was initially subdivided into Task Groups 116.1 for the Delta proper and 116.2 for the Rung Sat. Eighty of the new PBR river patrol boats went

to 116.1 and 40 to 116.2. In January 1968, the Squadron was enlarged to four task groups assigned to specific rivers: 116.1- Song Bassac, 116.2- Song Co Chien, 116.3- Song My Tho, and 116.4- Rung Sat Special Zone. In June, Task Group 116.5 was added to cover the Delta's upriver region near the Cambodian border. By late 1968, another 130 PBRs were assigned. River Patrol Squadron 5 became Flotilla Five in September and was reorganized into River Divisions with bases at: 51- Cah Tho/Binh Thuy, 52- Sa Dec (later Vinh Long), 53- My Tho, 54- Song Nha Be, 55- Danang (I CTZ). The divisions were subdivided into four or five sections of 10 PBRs each. PACV Division 107, with Patrol Air Cushion Vehicles, was attached to Task Force 116 in 1966. Helicopter Attack Squadron (Light) 3 was assigned to the Task Force in April 1967. It replaced Helicopter Combat Support Squadron 1, which had operated since June 1966. The Task Force was supported by Detachment GOLF with three SEAL platoons rotated from SEAL Team 1. Another unit was Mine Division 112 with 12 Mine Sweeping Boats (MSB). The last unit to be assigned to Task Force 116 was Strike Assault Boat Squadron 20 (STABRON) with 22 STABs in November 1969. Four LSTs were converted to repair and otherwise support the PBRs. The Task Force reached a peak strength of 258 craft backed by 25 UH-1B helicopters and 15 OV-10A aircraft. The force stood down in December 1970 and its craft, with the exception of the STABs, were turned over the VNN. Of the 14 Medals of Honor awarded to Navy personnel in the Vietnam War, three were awarded to two PBR crewmen, one posthumously, and a river assault officer.

While most inshore operations took place in the Mekong Delta, Task Force CLEARWATER (the only task force not to receive a number) was established in I CTZ on the northernmost rivers of South Vietnam. A PBR section was deployed to the Song Cua Dai from September to October 1967 to test their effectiveness. The NVA and VC were attacking Navy supply convoys on the Song Huong Giang (Perfume) and Song Cua Viet. PBR Division 55 was sent north by Task Force 116 in January 1968. The situation deteriorated and Task Force CLEARWATER was formed in February 1968. Most of Task Force 117's RAD 112 was attached to it along with PBR Division 55 and some LCM(6) landing craft converted to minesweepers. The more heavily armed riverine craft patrolled the Perfume River as the Dong Ha River Security Group while the PBRs served on the Cua Viet in the Hue River Security Group. CLEARWATER security missions continued until June 1970.

To further unbalance VC forces in the Delta, Operation SEALORDS (South-East Asia Lake, Ocean, River, and Delta Strategy) was initiated in October 1968. Commander, Naval Forces, Vietnam (NAVFORV)

appointed his deputy (called the "First SEALORD") to command this operation and its Task Force 194. The Task Force's assets were provided by Task Forces 115, 116, and 117 along with SEAL units. The SEALORDS campaign saw the establishment of "barriers" (marauding patrol boats and remote movement detecting sensors) along waterways paralleling the Cambodian border in the northern reaches of the Delta. The operation's goal was to more effectively interdict VC logistics efforts by intercepting water infiltration attempts as they entered the country from NVA base areas within the Cambodia sanctuary. Extremely effective, Task Force 194 was disestablished in June 1970.

The small craft employed by US Navy riverine, river patrol, and coastal patrol forces included modified landing craft, purpose-built patrol boats, and various auxiliary craft. Regardless, their design features took into account the lessons learned by the French in the late 1940s and early 1950s by their divisions navales d'assaut (Dinassauts or naval assault divisions). American riverine warfare craft, a new classification category established by the Navy on 14 August 1968, included:

ASPB	Assault Support Patrol Boat
ATC	Armored Troop Carrier
ATCH	Armored Troop Carrier (Helicopter)
CCB	Command and Communications Boat
LCMR	Landing Craft, Mechanized, Rocket
LLC	Salvage Craft
MON	Monitor (formerly LCM Monitor)
PACV	Patrol Air Cushion Vehicle
PBR	Patrol Boat, River
RPC	River Patrol Craft
SSB	SEAL Support Boat (two types, light and medium)
STAB	Strike Assault Boat (modification of the light SSB)
WPB	All-weather Patrol Boat (Coast Guard cutter)

Employed alongside these were several types of landing craft, landing ships, auxiliary service, and yard craft, in addition to those listed under RIVSUPRON 7:

Ammi	"Ammi" Pontoon Barge
LCM	Landing Craft, Mechanized (two types LCM(6), LCM(8))
LCVP	Landing Craft, Vehicle or Personnel
LCU	Landing Craft, Utility
MSB	Mine Sweeping Boat
YFNB	Covered Lighter, Large (self-propelled barge)
YFU	Harbor Craft, Utility
YLLC	Salvage Lift Craft, Light
YOG	Gasoline Barge, Self-propelled

References:
Croizat, Lt. Col. Victor. Vietnam River Warfare 1945-1975, London: Bradford Press,1986.
Cutler, Lt. Cdr. Thomas J. Brown Water, Black Berets: Coastal and Riverine Warfare in Vietnam, New York: Pocket Books, 1988.
Fulton, Maj. Gen. William B. Riverine Operations 1966-69, Washington, DC: Department of the Army, 1973.
Marolda, Edward J. By Sea, Air, and Land: An Illustrated History of the U.S. Navy and the War in Southeast Asia, Washington, DC: Naval Historical Center, 1994.
Schreadley, Cdr. R. L. From the Rivers to the Sea: The United States Navy in Vietnam, Annapolis, MD: Naval Institute Press, 1992.

A special thanks to Michael Green for helping with some of the photos.

A PBR Mk II makes a full-speed run with the crew scanning the river banks for enemy activity. This boat, conducting training in California, mounts international orange life preservers, often removed in combat. On many boats the Pathfinder LN 66 relative bearing search and navigation radar's antenna dome was painted light gray or even remained the original white.

A pair of PBR Mk IIs motor to their night patrol sector as the sun sets. The far boat's hull bottom is painted bright red, but most had solid olive green hulls.

A PBR Mk II crew searches a sampan. One of the boarding crew is armed with a 12-gauge semi-automatic shotgun, an excellent close-quarters weapon.

One of the most predominate weapons employed on riverine warfare and coastal patrol craft was the Browning .50-caliber HB-M2 machine gun (HB=Heavy Barrel). The ".50-cal" could be fitted to several types of mounts including the power-operated twin-mount on PBRs and PCFs (seen here from the business end on a PBR Mk II), single flexible mount, single turret mount, and "piggy-back" mounted atop a direct-fire 81mm mortar on PCFs and WPBs.

A PBR Mk II viewed from the bow. The dark lusterless olive green was an excellent color for these boats as it blended well with shoreline foliage and made it all but invisible on a moonless night. A black-painted boat was too dark and stood out on the water or the shoreline.

The engine compartment of the a PBR Mk II shows off its two General Motors 220-horsepower diesel engines. Due to long, rugged use, maintenance was an endless effort.

A stern view of an ATC. Judging from the barrel covers on the 20mm and .50-caliber guns and a pair of mops beside two resting crewmen without armor vests, it is safe to say that the craft is in a secure area. On the aft of the deckhouse bulkhead are white plastic fenders that would be placed over the side when docking, a red fire extinguisher, and a basket litter.

The ATC was the mainstay of the river force. A "Tango boat" could carry a rifle platoon plus attachments.

A rifle platoon re-embarks an ATC after searching a riverside hootch or the Lon Tau. This picture provides an excellent example of screening vegetation typically found along river banks.

Typical wet season terrain is demonstrated by this scene of a small tributary flanked by palms and flooded fields. A lone ATC checks out the apparently abandoned hootchs, except that the fields have been recently plowed.

"Tango boats" nose into a densely vegetated riverbank to disembark troops. A 16-ft. plastic assault boat is tied alongside.

A river assault division had one or two CCBs, which provided communications with all elements, higher headquarters, and supporting aircraft. Vietnamese sampans plying the waterways generally ignored combat operations.

While most of this late type CCB Mk II is painted gray, the bow plates and some other fittings are painted olive green. The red boxes serve to protect antenna mounts. Black rubber fenders are hung from the gunwales. A PBR Mk II is tied to the CCB's stern.

A Zippo torches riverbank vegetation in a effort to deny the VC future ambush positions.

While intended for inshore patrols PCF Swift boats were also used for river patrols. While possessing a 4-ft.10-in draft, they could be used effectively on the larger rivers.

10

The 81mm mortar crew on the fantail of a PCF Swift boat prepares to [fir]e the Mk 2 mortar. The white phosphorus (WP) round can cause [ca]sualties due to its bursting charge scattering burning phosphorus globs [an]d particles. "Willie Pete" was also used to start brush fires and produce [scr]eening smoke. The WP round is identified by a light green body, light red [an]d yellow bands, and yellow markings. High explosive rounds had an olive [dr]ab body with a yellow band and markings. Both men wear dungarees with [M1]952 armor vests. The gunner wears a Mk 2 talker helmet while the loader [wear]s a standard M1 steel helmet.

A bow view of a PCF Swift boat in its olive green colors. A 7.62mm M60 machine gun is retrofitted forward of the wheel house, not a standard fitting. While white hull numbers were the most common for visibility, black numbers were also used.

A PCF Swift boat pulls alongside a [we]ll-maintained Vietnamese junk for a [rou]tine inspection. The Swift has been ["ca]mouflaged" by spray painting a black ["w]orm-pattern" on its dark olive green. [Th]is is totally ineffective as it does [no]thing to break-up or disrupt its [out]line. From even a short range the [bo]at still appears to be solid dark green. [Th]e side windows were replaced with [ply]wood as they were blown out so [fre]quently that insufficient [rep]lacements were available.

A PACV bears its dragon teeth and evil orange eyes. Although difficult see, the eyes are shrouded by blac arched eyebrows. Unlike the eyes of Vietnamese junks, the "Dragon Boat" (a name given by Vietnames fishermen) eyes and teeth were intended to instill fear. A white U. NAVY is painted on the cabin's sid below the gun tub.

A Mine Sweeping Boat (MSB), crewed by six men, cruises with its sweeping gear stowed on the fantail. A .50-caliber machine gun is mounted in the stern gun tub while two .30-calibers were usually on the forecastle. The craft is painted the standard gray with a wooden hull bottom painted black. Note the white radar antenna dome. The MSB was 57.2 ft. (17.4m) long with a beam of 15.5 ft. (4.7m). Its two diesels pushed it at 12 knots.

Two medium SEAL Support Boa (SSB), their twin water jets propelli them at a moderate speed, are paint olive green and have their canv awnings erected. This was usua removed to lower its profile. The boat mounts a radar.

A SEAL squad departs for a night ambush patrol aboard a Boston Whaler or "Skimmer". The boat is olive green with the gunwales smeared with Delta mud due to constant debarking and reembarking on river banks. The boat's two 75-horsepower outboard engines are visible. The SEALs wear woodlands pattern camouflage uniforms while the boat coxswain wears olive green jungle fatigues. Skimmers were also used by IUWUs.

The 16-ft. Boston Whalers or Skimmers were often painted in four-color camouflage patterns, here in black, forest green, olive drab, and sand.

A Navy SEAL occupies an ambush site on a ca
bank. He is outfitted in a mismatched tiger-str
uniform and armed with a 5.56mm Mk 23 Mod 0 li
machine gun, better known as the Stoner 63.

An HAL(L)-3, the "Seawolves", UH-1B displays the squadron's insignia on the nose. The fire-breathing "hybrid" seawolf, the cross between a sea dragon and wolf, is blue with red claws, bears a red and yellow shield charged with a black spade, and banishes a black trident.

Both Navy and Army helicopters were employed to provide ae surveillance and fire support for riverine operations. Here a UH- Seawolf's door gunner searches for enemy activity.

A Navy Seawolf Huey lands on the gray-painted USS Benewah (APB-35). An Army Huey is in the background.

A Vietnamese Popular Force river outpost served to both place surveillance on river traffic and guard a local village from attack from the river. The bunker beneath the guard tower probably mounts a .30-caliber machine gun while the bunker to the left protected riflemen. The high barrier fence served mainly to protect the outpost from RPG-2 and RPG-7 rockets fired from passing boats, a form of protection from "drive-by" shootings. The red and yellow Vietnamese flag flew over all of these small outposts.

A VNN STCAN/FOM patrol boat sports the more or less standard Vietnamese river boat camouflage of light and dark olive drab, forest green, and gray painted in its distinctive foliage pattern. This blended well along river banks. Note that the canvas flaps over the cabin ports are painted in shades of gray on black. Ammunition cans for the .30-caliber machine gun are stowed behind the wheel house.

This bow view of a 16.9-meter Yabuta junk displays its eyes on the traditional red backing. The .50-caliber machine gun is protected by a shield. The junk itself is painted gray and the crew wears unusual gray uniforms rather than the normal black.

This poorly maintained Yabuta junk passes astern of a cargo ship awaiting its turn to enter the Long Tau, the main shipping channel connecting Vung Tau on the coast with inland Saigon, the country's main seaport. Navigating the Long Tau meant running a virtual gauntlet through the VC dominated Rung Sat Special Zone. Two National Police accompany the junk on its patrol.

A 11.5m motor junk extracts an ARVN reconnaissance patrol. Most motor junks were unarmed, but this one has a tripod-mounted .30-caliber M1919A4 machine gun (slightly modified M1919A4) on a wood platform at the bow. The eyes painted on all Vietnamese junks were meant to watch for danger and thus prevent harm to the crew.

A Yabuta junk's main armament was its single .30-caliber M1919A4 machine gun fitted to a locally fabricated mount. Most junk crewmen were informally "uniformed". The Yabuta was actually a Japanese design.

"Salty" is perhaps the best word to describe America's brown water sailors. Serving long days aboard small craft with few comfort amenities, distant from desk-bound officers, they viewed themselves as free-wheeling and independent from the spit and polish of the "big ship Navy". This Junk Force advisor wears Vietnamese black "pajamas", the same as the Vietnamese crewmen, and the Navy advisor's black beret adorned with a silver Junk Force badge. The badge is worn over the right temple French/Vietnamese style rather than over the left eye as was US practice.

Like virtually all riverine craft, this 50-ft. Assault Support Patrol Boat (ASPB) is painted solid dark olive green. Most fixtures and fittings were painted olive green as well. Weathering, incomplete repainting, spot painting, and battle damage repairs gave a worn and battered appearance to most riverine craft. Old automobile and jeep tires were commonly used as side fenders.

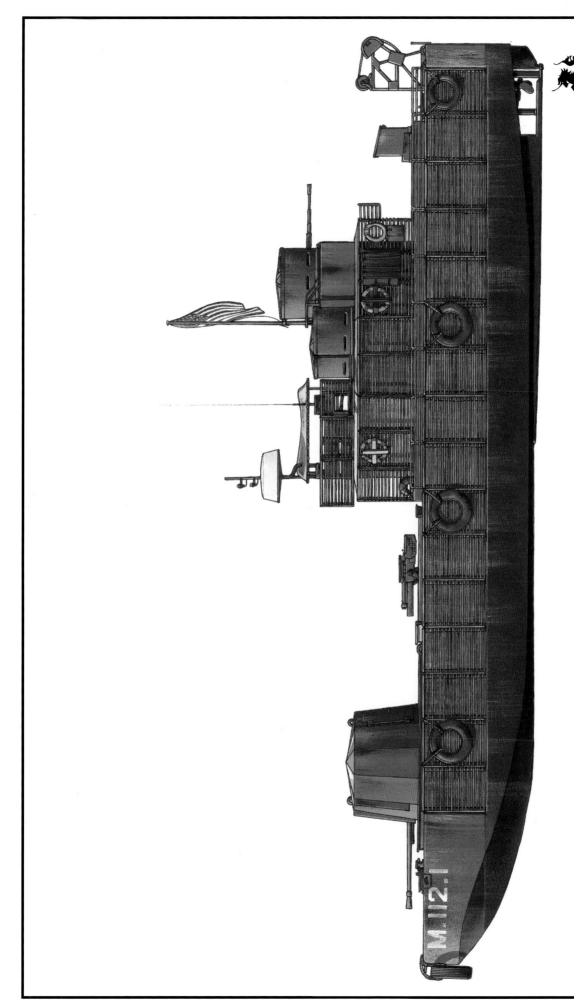

The 60-ft. monitor (MON), clad in its steel bar-armor, displays its formidable array of weapons. The barrels of 40mm, 20mm, .50-caliber, and .30-caliber weapons were often unpainted and gunmetal colored, almost black. The life preserver rings were international orange, but were sometimes sprayed olive green. Hull numbers, when applied near the bow, were white, although black letters and numbers were occasionally used.

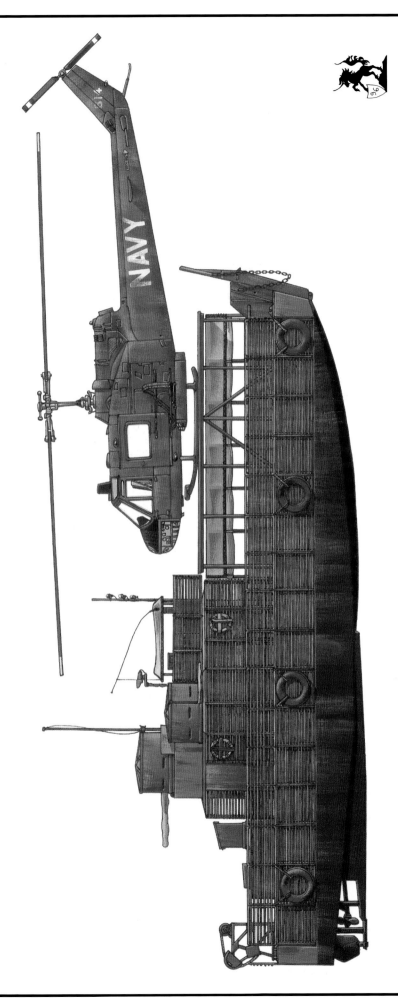

A UH-1B Huey helicopter has alighted aboard a 60-ft. Armored Troop Carrier (Helicopter) (ATCH). Helicopters were painted forest green, a much darker green than riverine crafts' olive green. What markings there were may have been the earlier white or more common black. The M60C machine guns were gunmetal with black feed covers. The 2.75-in. rocket pods were olive green . . Awnings were made of treated canvas and painted brownish green, but sometimes painted the same color as the boat. Gun barrel covers were made of canvas (canvas shades varied greatly from brownish green to dark olive green).

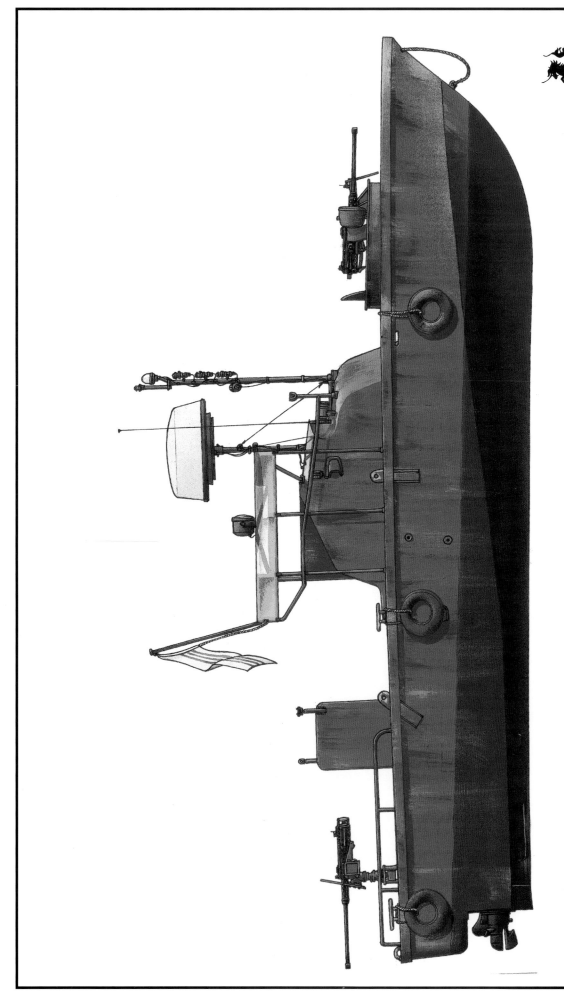

Some 32-ft. PBR Mk II's beneath the waterline hull were painted bright red, but solid olive green hulls were more common. US Navy small craft were fitted with the full array of running lights as required by international rules. These were of course not turned on during operations, but used during Stateside training and in harbors. Boats over 26 ft. in length were required to mount white lights near the bow and stern and at least one white light on a masthead. When towing or under tow, two or three masthead lights were required as seen on this masthead.

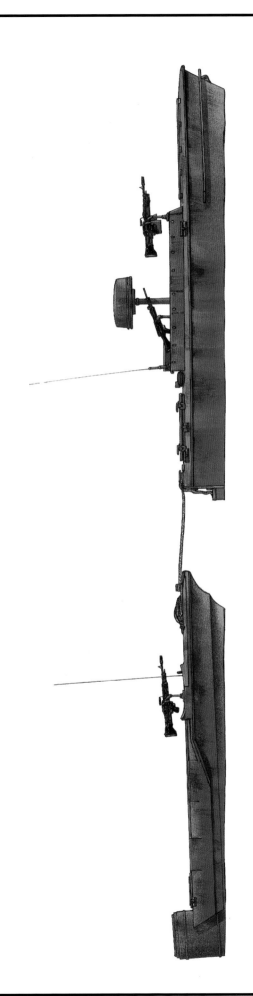

A Strike Assault Boat (STAB) tows a Light SEAL Support Boat (LSSB). The STAB's LN 66 radar dome may have been painted olive green, light gray, or left in its original commercial white. The paint often flaked off. The STAB mounts a 7.62mm M60 machine gun forward and a 5.56mm Mk 23 MOD 0 (Stoner 63) machine gun abeam. Being under 26 ft. in length, the only lights these boats were required to display was a white light near the stern, but both boats have had theirs removed.

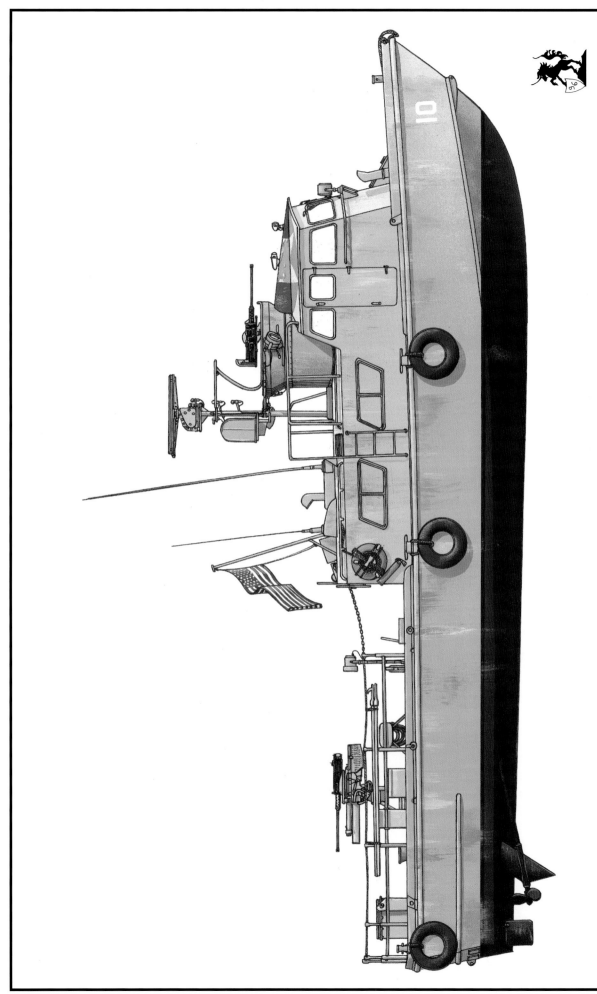

Although used mainly offshore, 50-ft. PCF Mk I Swift boats were sometimes painted olive green like riverine boats, but this one is in gray as other open water craft. The 81mm Mk 2 mortar may have been painted olive green or gray, but the HB-M2 .50-caliber machine gun was gunmetal. Virtually all fittings and equipment were gray. All craft over 26 ft. in length were required to have side lights mounted on the cabin: red on port (left), green on starboard (right). A white star was painted atop of most US Navy riverine craft.

The 39-ft. Patrol Air Cushion Craft (PACV) were painted olive green. The rubber skirts were black. Red and white dragon's teeth were often painted on the bow skirt leading to their "Dragon Boat" nickname. Orange eyes with black eyebrows adorned the bows above the skirt. PACVs carried the same running lights as small craft, but were also required to mount an all-round flashing yellow light on the radar mast (not used during operations).

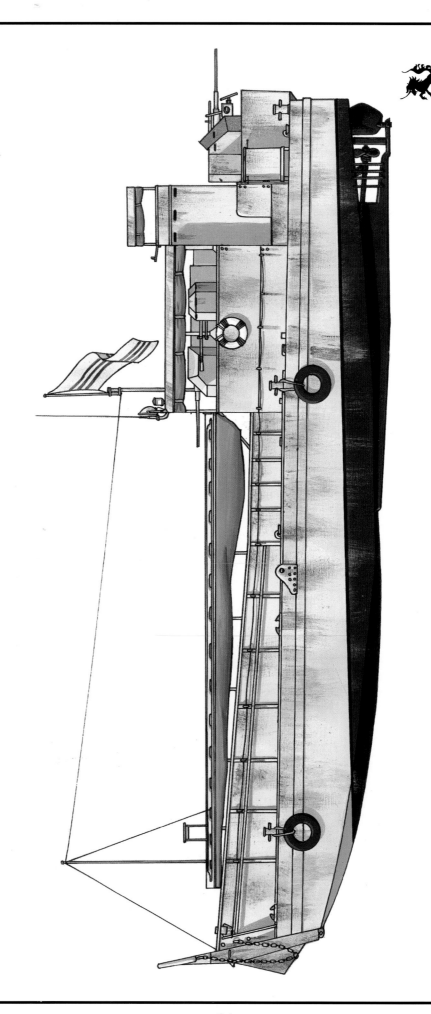

This VNN armored Landing Craft, Medium (LCM(6)) is gray, which tended to be well weathered. Camouflage painting of VNN riverine craft was more common than in the US Navy. While there were no standard patterns, the light and dark olive drab, forest green, and gray foliage pattern were often employed as pictured on the STCAN/FOM in the color section. VNN junks, coastal patrol craft, and other oceangoing craft were gray.

THE BOATS

The ASPB was an armored, high-speed (when compared to other riverine craft) boat employed for escort, interdiction, surveillance, fire support, base defense, and mine sweeping. Intended as the river assault squadron's "destroyer", 16 "Alpha boats" were assigned. It was armed with a turret-mounted 20mm automatic cannon atop the deckhouse and twin .50-caliber machine guns forward plus a direct-fire mm mortar in the stern cockpit (not visible here). Some had two 40mm automatic grenade launchers or 7.62mm machine guns mounted forward of the deckhouse.

The 35-ton, 50-ft. (15m) ASPB was crewed by six men and could make 16 knots. The only riverine warfare craft designed specifically for the purpose, it was plagued with problems. The freeboard was too low and the open aft cockpit was exposed to enemy fire and grenades. It possessed hydraulic steering highly susceptible to damage by gun fire. Its armor was far too light resulting in high casualty levels among crews. They were introduced in September 1967.

The armored Landing Craft, Vehicle or Personnel (LCVP) was a modification of the standard LCVP used since 1942. The armored version was used for troop transport, fire support, and mine sweeping. The "Papa boat" was 36 ft. long with a 10-ft. 6-in. beam. Modifications included armor plating on its plywood hull and a troop compartment cover. This one, armed with two forward .50-caliber machine guns plus two 7.62mm in the aft, is extracting a SEAL patrol.

The Landing Craft, Mechanized Mk VI or LCM(6) was the workhorse of the Navy's landing craft fleet. Developed in 1943, the "Mike boat" was 56 ft. (24m) in length with a 14-ft. (4.2m) beam. It displaced 58 tons with a 3-ft. 8-in. draft and had a 10 knot speed. It could carry a tank or 155mm howitzer or 60,000 lbs. of cargo or 60 troops. It had a three or four-man crew. The Mike boat provided the basis for most of the riverine craft and were heavily modified to serve special purposes. Unmodified, they still served in many support roles.

The ATC was the most numerous of the riverine craft with 26 assigned to a river assault squadron. Based on a modified LCM(6), it could carry 40 combat-equipped troops. It was well-armed with its seven-man crew manning a 20mm cannon (aft turret), two .50-caliber (side turrets) and up to four 7.62mm Mk 21 machine guns or two 40mm automatic grenade launchers. In 1968 they were upgraded with 20mm's in the two side turrets and a 40mm Mk 19 automatic grenade launcher in the aft turret.

Under Project Douche some ATCs had two high-pressure water pump cannons, as used on fire fighting boats, with a 300-meter range. They were used to destroy shoreline bunkers, wash away camouflage, and fight fires on other boats. Capable of generating 3,000 pounds per square inch, a "Douche boat" could dissolve concrete at close-range.

Side blisters were fitted to the ATC to provide additional buoyancy due to increased displacement (66 tons) and added protection from gun fire. The steel-bar armor was intended to protect from the shaped-charge projectiles of RPG-7 rocket launchers and recoilless rifles. The troop compartment was covered with a canvas awning for protection from grenades and the blistering sun. The main problem of the ATC and other river assault craft built around the LCM(6) was its slow 6-8 knot speed caused by added armor, weapons, and other modifications. They were known as "Tango boats" due to their identifying hull code.

The monitor was the "battleship" of the river assault squadron with five assigned. Its large forward turret mounted a 40mm cannon and .50-caliber machine gun (to the right of the 40mm) while the wheel house turrets had the same armament as the ATC, a 20mm and two .50 calibers. The open midships well-deck between the forward turret and wheel house had an 81mm direct fire mortar and two side-mounted 7.62mm Mk 21 machine guns.

In 1968 improvements were made to newly constructed monitors, ATCs, and CCBs under Program 5. For the monitors the forward 40mm cannon was replaced by a 105mm M49 howitzer (as used on Marine Corps LVTH-6 amphibian tractors). Modifications included additional steel-bar armor. Monitors, depending on the armament, generally had an 11-man crew. They were 60 ft. (18m) long, had a 17.5-ft. (5.5m) beam, and displaced 75 tons. MONs, CCBs, and ASPBs were fitted with surface search and navigation radars. All riverine craft had FM radios.

Another modification of the monitor was the removal of much of its armament and the addition of two flame guns. While there were variants of secondary armament, this one mounts a single .50-caliber machine gun turret atop the wheel house. Nicknamed "Zippos", their main purpose was to defeat bunkers, burn away shoreline foliage, and provide a psychological weapon.

The "flagship" of the river assault divisions was the CCB, "Commandement", a term borrowed from the French. The squadron had two, one for each of its two division commanders. They were based on the monitor, but lacked the 81mm mortar. It had two 7.62mm Mk 21 machine guns amidships and retained the turreted 40mm, 20mm, and two .50-calibers. The former mortar well deck had an armored housing module outfitted as a floating command center with radios, map tables, and staff work spaces.

A Program 5 CCB Mk II was intended for river assault squadrons. It mounts only a .50-caliber machine gun forward and the same after armament of an ATC, which is obscured by camouflage nets. These served more to provide shade than tactical camouflage. Note the large number of radio antennas.

The Program 5 ATCH was an ATC fitted with an armored helicopter landing platform above the troop compartment making them "the world's smallest aircraft carriers". On most versions, the platform was slightly lower being level with the deck on which the man is standing. This could accept a single UH-1 Huey helicopter and aided in the evacuation of wounded and re-supply of ammunition and supplies; the Mekong Delta was notoriously short of suitable helicopter landing zones ashore.

The refueller, one per river assault squadron, was a heavily modified ATC fitted with armor-protected diesel fuel storage tanks, fuel transfer pumps, and extensive bar-armor on the bow. Besides normal ATC armament, fitted to the bow were two .50-caliber HB-M2 machine guns mounted in M1 cupolas off of M48A2 Patton tanks.

River assault force craft were mostly painted a standard lusterless, dark olive green. A large white star adorned an upper surface to allow it to be identified by aircraft. The American flag served the same purpose. A white boat identification code was painted on the bows, stern, and an upper surface. The prefix letter identified the type of boat (A- ASPB, C- CCB, M-MON, T- ATC, Z- flame boat). This was followed by a two or three-digit number identifying the river assault division (91, 92, 111, 112, 121, 131, 132, 151, 152). The first two numbers (first number in the case of 91 and 92) additionally identified the division's parent river assault squadron. A one or two-digit suffix number identified the boat within the division.

The vendible PBR river patrol boat was widely used, not only for its intended purpose, but as a hunter-killer. These nimble little boats could enter portions of the rivers that only sampans could navigate. All models had fiberglass hulls and two 220-horsepower diesel engines propelling two Jacuzzi water jets to make them highly maneuverable. This is an PBR Mk II and could reach speeds up to 28 knots in less than a foot of water since they had no rudder or propellers. By reversing its water jets, it could stop in its own length at full speed. At slow speeds it drew 2 ft. of water. They did have a problem with dirty water and vegetation debits clogging the water jets.

The PBR Mk I was developed in 1965 and first reached Vietnam in March 1966. The boat was based on an existing commercial design thus speeding the production of the 120 Mk Is. They were 31 ft. long with a 10-ft. 6-in. beam. The crew of four manned a twin .50-caliber machine gun forward and on the stern was a .50-caliber machine gun often duel-mounted with a 40mm grenade launcher. The 40mm might be on a pedestal amidships. A 7.62mm machine gun was provided to mount on either side. Slightly slower than the Mk II, the Mk I could do 25 knots. This one took four hits around its hull number.

These PBR Mk IIs show the main difference between the two marks. The gun tub is located further forward, it has a larger cockpit fairing, and there is a pronounced aluminum gunwale to protect the fiberglass hull from damage when junks were boarded. They were also a foot longer than the Mk I, had a 11-ft. 8-in. beam, and had 2,200 lbs. (1,000kg) greater displacement. Armament remained the same, but additional machine guns were often added. Eighty Mk IIs were delivered in 1967.

In 1969, 20 modified Light SEAL Support Craft (LSSC) were deployed to Vietnam as Strike Assault Boats (STAB) and assigned to Strike Assault Boat Squadron 20. The STAB had an aluminum, ceramic armor-lined hull that was 26 ft. 2 in. long with a beam of 10 ft. 4 inches. It had a 3-ft. 9-in. draft and displaced 15,000 lbs. (8,600kg). Powered by two prop-driven 350-horsepower gasoline engines, the STAB could achieve 45 knots. Its crew of four had three M60 machine guns and a 40mm Mk 20 automatic grenade launcher. It had mounted a radar, but these were removed in Vietnam. All STABs were returned to the States in 1970.

Numerous experimental projects were conducted by riverine and patr units. One of these was the Minesweeping Drone (MSD) tested in ea 1969. The 23-ft. MSD was maneuvered into position by a two-man cre who were picked up by an ASPB. An operator on the ASPB then steer the MSD via a radio-control transmitter, similar to those used with radi controlled model airplanes. Either a bottom drag chain or moored-mi sweeping gear was towed by the MSD at 10 knots and proved to l effective. Note that pairs of four-tube 2.75-inch rocket pods, as used helicopters, have been retrofitted to the ASPB's forward turret.

The PCF or "Swift" Mk I insho patrol boat was another adapte commercial design, in this case from boat used to deliver men and materi to Gulf of Mexico offshore oil rigs. Th over 100 Swift boats were used f coastal patrol duties by Task Force 11 They were 50-ft. long and had a 13-6-in. beam with an aluminum hu Their two 475-horsepower diese could drive them at 25 knots. Th displaced only 19 tons and 31/2 ft. water. Armament was comprized of twin mounted .50-caliber machine g atop the wheel house and an 81m direct-fire mortar dual mounted with .50-caliber on the fantail. The first these six-man crewed boats arrived October 1967.

The WPB Coast Guard all-weather patrol boat was intended as a search and rescue cutter, but they served with Coast Guard Division 12 under the Navy's Coastal Surveillance Force in July 1965. The 26 82-ft. WPBs had a 17-ft. 3-in. beam. Their 67.5 tons displacement had draft of 6-ft. 5 inches. Its 600-horsepower diesel could push the cutter to 18 knots. It was a sea-going ship with a steel hull and aluminum superstructure. The 11-man crew served an 81mm direct-fire mortar dual mounted with a .50-caliber on the bow and four single .50 calibers on the fantail.

Three Rocket Support Ships (LFR-[9], 525, 536) provided shore bombardment support (before 1 January 1969, Landing Ship Medium, Rocket [LSMR]). The USS St. Francis River (LFR-525) was a former Landing Craft Infantry (Large) (LCI(L)). It was armed with eight semi-automatic 5-inch barrage rocket launchers, a 5-inch gun (here aimed to port), and two dual-mounted 40mm cannons. The LFR was 211 ft. long with a 34-ft. 5-in. beam and displaced 1,280 tons. It had a 138-man crew. A similar Inshore Fire Support Ship (IFS-1) also served.

The most advanced craft used by the Navy in Vietnam was the USS Tucumcari (PGH-2), one of two Patrol Gunboats, Hydrofoil built. Both, the other was the USS Flagstaff (PGH-1), were assigned to Task Force 115, but were not too effective in rough seas and demanded constant maintenance. The 13-man crew manned a 40mm cannon and three twin .50-caliber machine guns. The PGHs were 82 ft. (24.40 m) in length (12 m) and had a maximum speed of 50 knots.

In February 1967 three Patrol Gunboats were assigned to Task Force 115. This one is the class's name ship, the USS Asheville (PG-84). The others were the Gallup (PG-85) and Crockett (PG-88). The 37 knot, 165-ft. boats were armed with a 3-inch Mk 34 gun (with Mk 64 fire control radar) forward, a 40mm cannon aft, an 81mm mortar, and two .50-caliber machine guns.

The smallest craft used in riverine operations was the commercially made [1]2-ft. fiberglass skimmer, here powered by a small Mercury outboard motor.

THE WEAPONS

The weapons employed on riverine warfare and coastal patrol craft were intended for three types of targets: enemy fortifications, troops, and unarmored small craft. Engaging enemy combatant ships and air defense were not primary considerations. They were required to possess a high rate of fire and, for the most part, have a flat trajectory to allow direct, line-of-sight fire.

The uncluttered stern view of a monitor indicates that it had recently arrived in-country. This one appears to be a latter model with side-mounted 20mm cannons (rather than .50-calibers) and an aft-mounted 40mm grenade launcher (rather than a 20mm). The 20mm Mk 2 automatic cannon was mounted as a flexible gun in the manually-operated Mk 48 turret of ATCs, monitors, and CCBs as well as powered turrets on the ASPB. The Swiss-designed Oerlikon was originally intended as a ship-board antiaircraft gun and also used on fighter aircraft. Its high explosive shells could be fired at a rate of 550 rounds per minute to a maximum effective range of 2,000 yards. It was fed by a 60-round drum magazine.

The 40mm M1 automatic cannon was mounted in the manually-operated forward turret on monitors and CCBs. The Swedish-designed Bofors was originally used as a ship-board antiaircraft gun on single, twin, and quad mounts. Its high explosive and armor-piercing projectiles could be fired at a rate of 120 rounds per minute to a maximum effective range of 5,000 yards. It was fed by four-round clips. A .50-caliber machine gun was mounted in the turret to the 40mm's right. Note the vision slits in the turret's sides.

The 7.62mm M60 machine gun was widely used aboard PBRs and other craft. As the standard infantry machine gun it was normally used on bipod, but could be mounted on a tripod. This M60 is mounted on a 16-foot Boston Whaler, or "Skimmer", used by SEALs and other Navy forces as base defense boat. The M60 fired at a rate of 600 rounds per minute. As flexible gun it had a effective range of 800 meters.

The World War II era Browning .30-caliber M1919A4 light machine gun was rebarreled by the Navy to fire the 7.62mm NATO cartridge used in the M60 machine gun. Fitted with a closed-prong flash suppresser, the Navy designated it the Mk 21 Mod 0. This one is mounted on the side of a monitor's mortar well-deck. The mortar's olive drab plastic cartridge tubes are seen to the left. The Browning fired at a rate of 450-500 rounds per minute and had the same effective range as an M60.

The 81mm Mk 2 direct-fire mortar was "piggy-back" mounted with a .50-caliber machine gun and found on WPBs (as here), PCFs, and monitors. The "eighty-one" could fire high explosive and white phosphorus smoke rounds by direct fire to over 1,000 yards. With an observer, it could be fired up to 3,940 yards, but this was seldom done. It could be trigger-fired at 0 rounds per minute or drop-fired at 18 rounds per minute. The Browning .50-caliber HB-M2 machine gun (HB=Heavy Barrel) was one of the most predominate weapons employed on riverine warfare and coastal patrol craft. It could also be fitted to other types of mounts including the power-operated twin-mount on PBRs and PCFs, single flexible mount, and single turret mount. "SAT-CONG" is Vietnamese for "Kill the Cong". The gunner wears a Mk 2 talker helmet allowing the use of an intercom headset.

A SEAL Squad practices with the Honeywell 40mm Mk 18 Mod 0 grenade launcher. Usually mounted on PBRs, it could be mounted on an M60 machine gun's M122 tripod for ground use. It was hand-crank operated and had an effective range of only about 300 meters. It used the same low-velocity rounds as the M79, but were belted. It was a devastating weapon when used against wooden sampans and junks. The weapon was later replaced by the Mk19 Mod 0.

This Zippo flame boat mounts two M10-8 flame guns (as used on the Army's M132A1 armored flamethrower) aft of the 40mm turret, but later versions had them mounted on the bow without a 40mm. The flame guns were served by well-armored tanks holding 1,000 liters of thickened napalm fuel. They had a 150-meter range.

A 5-inch spin-stabilized rocket is launched from a semi-automatic launcher aboard the USS St. Francis River (LFR-525). The launch tube returned to vertical after firing to allow reloading by an automatic loader beneath it. The launchers could be laid by remote control thus eliminating the need to expose crewmen on deck. An LFR could fire 380 rockets in one minute to range of 10,000 yds. (9,000m).

Individual small arms were just as important as the larger caliber weapons. Here two of the most common shoulder weapons are fired at shoreline targets by brown water sailors, the new 5.56mm M16A1 rifle and the Korean War era .30-caliber M2 carbine. The M16A1 used a 20-round magazine while the carbine had a 30-round. Both fired semi and full-automatic.

An ammunition handler removes a 5-inch Mk 7 spin-stabilized rocket from its ready rack to place it in an automatic loader. The fuse tip, rotating and base bands are brass; the warhead is olive drab with a red nose and white markings, the rocket motor is light gray with black markings, and the rocket nozzle protector cap is red with a gray steel retaining band.

Three Patrol Air Cushion Vehicles (PACV or ACV) were introduced in late 1966. They were assigned to Task Force 116's PACV Division 107. The 5-ton "Dragon Boats" were British-made Winchester SR.N5 hovercrafts. They were 39 ft. long and 24 ft. wide. Powered by an aircraft engine, they could achieve up to 70-knot speeds across water and swamps. They could also climb over 4-ft. obstacles and travel across comparatively flat, dry land. Armament varied, but most had twin .50-caliber machine guns in the above-cabin gun tub and single .50-cals in the side ports. It could carry over a dozen passengers.

The Bell UH-1B Iroquois, or more popularly, Huey, light attack helicopter was used by Helicopter Attack Squadron (Light) 3, the "Seawolves". HA(L)-3 operated out of Vinh Long. The squadron's 22 choppers mounted an XM16 armament system consisting of twin M60C machine guns and a four-tube 2.75-inch rocket pod on both sides. An M60D machine gun was mounted in both doors and the door gunners also had an M79 grenade launcher. The usual white Navy markings have been painted over on this chopper.

The UH-1B helicopters used by the Navy were furnished by the Army and were still Army property. They had a four-man crew. They were 53 ft. long with a 44-ft. diameter main rotor and had a maximum cruising speed of 138 miles per hour. The normal color scheme was solid dark olive green, white or black (later) markings, and an anti-glare matte black upper nose. The close-up of an early Seawolf squadron insignia is all white on the Huey's matte black nose.

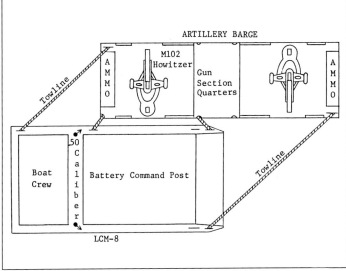

The Army constructed six artillery barges (enough for two batteries) by welding small pontoons together at Cam Ranh Bay on which two 105mm M102 howitzers were mounted. Each barge was towed by an Army LCM(8) landing craft of the 1097th Transportation Company (Medium Boat).

VIETNAMESE CRAFT

The Vietnamese Navy (VNN) employed a collection of former French, old US, and modern US river and coastal craft alongside modified junks and a few indigenous-built ships. Virtually all US riverine and coastal patrol craft remaining in Vietnam were transferred to the VNN in 1970-71 under the Small Craft Assets, Training and Turnover of Resources (SCATTOR) and Accelerated Turnover to the Vietnamese (ACTOR) programs.

The American-built ASPB was intended to replace the French-bu[ilt] STCAN/FOM (Services Technique des Constructions et Arme[es] Navales/France Outre Mer- the French Government organizatio[n] responsible for naval construction, FOM means it was built overseas). [It] was less reverently known to the Americans as the "stay-can" and to th[e] French as the vedatte ("outpost"). Used by the VNN until the war's end, th[e] STCAN/FOM had a 36-ft. (11m) steel hull. Its eight-man crew was protecte[d] by light armor and manned a turreted .50-caliber and three .30-calib[er] machine guns (in the side blisters and in one of the two tubs atop the whe[el]house. It was slow at only 10 knots.

Less widely used was the Frenc[h] modified armored Landing Cra[ft] Vehicle or Personnel (LCVP), [a] modification of the standard LCV[P] used since 1943. The armored versio[n] was used for troop transport, fi[re] support, and mine sweeping. Th[e] "Papa boat" was 36 ft. long with a 10-[ft.] 6-in. beam. Modifications included lig[ht] armor plating on its plywood hull, tro[op] compartment cover, and weapon[s]. These included a forward 20m[m] cannon and two .30-caliber machi[ne] guns in the aft side blisters. An VN[N] LCM(6) is in the background.

The River Assault Group 27 of the VNN operated the River Patrol Craft (RPC) from Mthyo. The RPC was designed to replace some of the older French craft and equipped with two twin .50-caliber and one .30-caliber machine guns.

The French-modified armored LCM(6) was used in the same mann[er] as the US ATC, but was significantly less armored. Its seven-man cre[w] operated three 20mm cannons and two .50-calibers, all in aft positio[n] protected by turrets and shields.

VNN LCM(6) monitors mounted [t]he same armament as their armored [L]CM(6)s, but with the addition of a [2]0mm cannon turret on the bow. A .50-[c]aliber machine gun is mounted beside [th]e 40mm. Note the camouflage [p]attern described in the color section.

This VNN armored LCM(6) shows the positioning of the weapons with [2]0mm in the aft turret, 20mm turrets on both sides (aft of the tent-like [aw]ning), and a .50-caliber firing port (no weapon) on both sides of the wheel [ho]use. An observer's seat is mounted on a tripod mast to allow observation [o]ver the river bank, a common modification on VNN riverine craft. Ex-[Fr]ench commandements were also used by the VNN.

The VNN Coastal Force maintained 28 coastal groups operating some [6]00 junks of all sizes. Most were wood-hulled, motorized junks; some with [sa]ils. Only command junks and 16.9-meter Yabuta junks (shown here) were [ar]med with a .50-caliber and .30-caliber machine gun. The Yabuta also had [a] 60mm mortar. Others (10-13m) had only the crew's individual weapons. [H]ere the .50-cal is on the bow, but may be switched with the .30-caliber.

The armed Yabuta junks mounted a 60mm M19 mortar amidships on a simple sandbag platform. The accuracy of firing an indirect fire mortar from one moving ship at another, and considering the projectile's long, slow flight time, sea swells, and stiff sea breezes, is virtually impossible to calculate. The 60mm was mainly used for firing illumination flares out to almost 2,000 yds. allowing the identification, and if necessary, the engagement of VC junks.

Vietnamese Army troops land a 21/2-ton cargo truck from an LCM(6). In the background is a VNN Landing Ship, Medium (LSM). The 203-ft. LS displaced 1,095 tons. It mounted two 40mm and four 20mm cannons. This is but one example of large VNN World War II era landing ships; they also use Landing Ships, Tank (LST) and Landing Ship, Infantry, Large (LSIL), known as a LCI(L) in the US Navy.

The Tuy Dong (HQ-04) was a VNN Sea Force patrol vess formerly used by the French and earlier by the US Navy as submarine chaser (PC). The 170-ft. vessel was armed with a inch Mk 22 gun, a 40mm cannon, and four 20mm cannons. Th PCs were used for offshore patrols to intercept Nor Vietnamese junks and to support the VNN Coastal Force junk

The PGM patrol motor gunboat was used by the VNN for offshore patrols. This one is the Dienh Hai (HQ-610) (The HQ hull number prefix on all VNN ships meant Hai Qu,n- Navy). The American-built 31-meter long boat with a 6.40-meter beam was powered by two 1,900-horsepower diesels to 17 knots. It was armed with a 40mm and two 20mm cannons, and two .50-calibers.

RIVERINE BASES

Riverine operations in the Mekong Delta were launched from floating bases positioned offshore or in large river estuaries.

The USS Askari (ARL-30) was a landing craft repair ship, a converted LST. Alongside are Ammi barges, ATCs, monitors, and LCM(6)s (an ATC is undergoing repairs on an Ammi). Up to one-third of a river assault squadron's craft might be undergoing repairs at any one time.

A self-propelled barracks barge, the USS Benewah (APB-35) alongside the USS Montrose (APA-212), an attack transport. The Benewah was the flagship of the Mobile Riverine Force. The 328-ft. ship was armed with four 4.2-inch mortars, two quad 40mm cannons, two twin 20mm cannons, and ten 7.62mm machine guns. Over 5,000 landings were made on Benewah's single helicopter pad in its first year of operation. The pad was white with red markings and numbers. Tied up alongside the Montrose are two Ammi barges, LCM(6)s, a CCB, an ATC, two LCVPs, and other small craft.

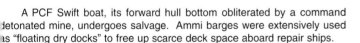

A PCF Swift boat, its forward hull bottom obliterated by a command detonated mine, undergoes salvage. Ammi barges were extensively used as "floating dry docks" to free up scarce deck space aboard repair ships.

Mobile Base II was built in the States on four Ammi barges to provide repair and overhaul for PBRs and ATSBs. It included such niceties as an air conditioned mess, comfortable quarters, and laundry. It was based in the Song Vam Co Tay at Tam An. Here a Navy UH-1B helicopter lands on the maintenance section while all hands hold a formation on the barracks section.

The USS Krishma (ARL-38) was one of two landing craft repair ships deployed to Vietnam. In July 1970 it was damaged by a mine exploded beneath it, but did not sink. The ARL had a crew of 190 and was armed with two quad 40mm gun mounts.

Two self-propelled barracks barges supported the Mobile Riverine Force. This is the USS Colleton (APB-36). The APBs were extensively modified LSTs capable of berthing 1,300 personnel. Each was home for an infantry battalion and a river assault squadron. Note the two helicopter pad configurations on the ATCHs.

A water-eye view of the USS Colleton with its river assault squadron moored alongside. APBs were painted olive green.

A self-propelled barracks barge arrives in Vietnam. It almost appears unusual as APBs were seldom seen without Ammi pontoons and hordes of riverine ...aft alongside.

A monitor and ATC moored to an Ammi pontoon alongside ...barracks ship. This view of a monitor shows the 40mm turret's ...t hatch.

The cargo deck of a Landing Craft, Utility (LCU-1484) being hosed down. The LCUs, known as LCT(6)s during World War II, were used to transport vehicles and heavy cargo in base support operations. Twin 20mm cannons can be seen flanking the wheel house.

41

RIVERINE OPERATIONS

A mobile riverine operation was a complex affair involving the orchestration of numerous US and Vietnamese Navy river assault units, Army ground units, Army aviation, Air Force close air support, and frequently, Vietnamese Army or territorial forces. Graphically depicted here is an example riverine operation and its search and clear operation ashore. The force departs from the Mobile Riverine Base (MRB) (A), as far as 50 kilometers from the objective area, before first light. The MRB is secured by patrol boats and elements ashore (B). A floating fire support base is established across the river from the objective area to support the main assault and blocking forces (C). The main assault force, escorted by ASPBs and monitors, moves up a tributary from the main river (D). As t assault force lands (E), blocking forces (US or Vietnamese) (F) a inserted on landing zones (LZ) by helicopter to seal the objective area a prevent the enemy from escaping. As the assault force sweeps toward objectives (G), ASAPs and monitors patrol to engage fleeing enemy (F A reaction force is on standby to reinforce, block, or pursue as required (Once the operation is completed, the ATCs that delivered it or other cr link-up with the assault force at the objectives (J). The fire support a blocking forces are withdrawn and all forces return to their bases for re maintenance, and to plan the next operation.

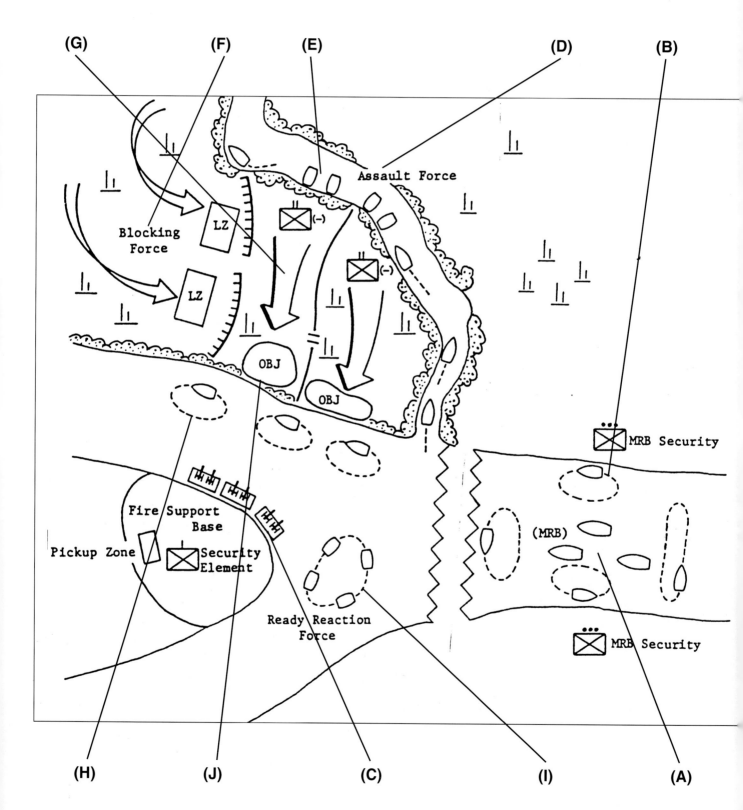

(A) A column of ATCHs depart its Mobile Riverine Base for its area of operations.

(B) Landing Craft, Personnel, Large (LCPL) were employed by Inshore Undersea Warfare Units (IUWU) 1 to 5 for harbor defense and surveillance. Swimmers, floating mines, and suicide boats were constant fears. The tiger jaws were white and red.

(C) Besides artillery mounted on Ammi barges, the Army provided XM6 helicopter-transportable platforms from which a 105mm M102 howitzer could be fired. The platforms were made of aluminum with plywood decks. There was an adjustable leg at each corner allowing the platform to rest in several feet of mud and water. They weighed 7,300 lbs. and measured 22 ft. to a side. The M102 had a 11,500-meter range.

(D) ATCs, escorted by a monitor, plow up a vegetation-choked tributary to a landing site.

(E) Lightly equipped to the short duration of search and clear operations, Mobile Riverine Force soldiers off-load an ATC.

(F) This ARVN unit, accompanied by its American advisors, prepares to move out to its blocking positions.

(G) A radioman and rifleman cross a drainage ditch as their platoon "sweeps" towards its objective.

(H) A monitor searches the river bank for fleeing VC as the landing force sweeps in from behind.

(I) A reaction force ATC waits to be called to action.

(J) Vietnamese Marines, who often took part in riverine search and clear operations, are retrieved from low tide mud flats by Swift boats. Rope nets were suspended from the bows to allow boarding.

A Navy gunner sweeps the river bank with a .50-caliber HB-M2 machine gun aboard an ATC. The gun station is protected by ceramic armor panels.

A monitor follows in the wake of a river assault column's last ATC to over the rear.

VNN riverine craft were often employed to support US riverine assault operations. Here two STCAN/FOMs and an LCM(6) turn up a river tributary to secure a flank.

PACV hovercrafts often supported riverine operations by patrolling tributaries and sweeping across marshland and rice paddies to intercept fleeing VC.

An Army UH-1B searches for enemy movement along a brush line. The VC were forced to use every bit of vegetation for hiding places. The white bar on the pilots' compartment probably identifies this armed Huey as a company or platoon commander's.

A dual-mounted 40mm Mk 1 cannon aboard USS Jennings County (LST-846) on the Bassac River provides fire support to units ashore. The 40mm cannons were fed by four-round clips. The gun crew wears M1952 armor vests. The sailor to the right wears a life vest over his body armor.

Agent Orange defoliant is sprayed on riverbank vegetation from an LCM(6) to prevent the enemy from using it for an ambush site. A gasoline pump powers the sprayer. Gasoline was also sprayed in the same manner and ignited by throwing trip flares into the drenched vegetation.

Struggling through sucking river muck, an M60 machine gunner demonstrates the difficulties of moving by foot through the Mekong Delta. was some of the most difficult terrain encountered in Vietnam.

One advantage of the PCF was its high wheel house and machine gun tub permitting good observation and fire over river banks.

The PBR river patrol boat was the most frequently seen patrol craft in the Mekong Delta. A crewman fires into a suspicious clump of vegetation on the riverside.

Besides the PBR, other small craft were used for river patrols in vicinity of floating bases. This LCPL mounts .50-caliber machine guns on the bow and ern with .30-calibers on the sides.

An officer briefs two petty officers 1st class (normal rating for P[...] captains) on an upcoming patrol in the northern portion of the Rung [...] Special Zone. The petty officers wear olive green short-sleeve fatigues w[...] black-on-OG U.S. NAVY and name tapes over the pockets and black-on-[...] rating marks on the left sleeve only.

The PACV was also used for river patrols. Its disadvantage in this role was its inability to exit the river over banks higher than 4 feet. Its loud roar was channeled down the river warning of its approach.

Helicopters frequen[...] accompanied river patr[...] scouting for enemy acti[...] ashore and searching [...] suspicious sampans. Her[...] Seawolf checks out [...] sampan hiding un[...] overhanging trees in [...] stream mouth.

A Seawolf aircraft commander scans a riverside village. He wears an M1952 armor vest and a dark green APH5 flying helmet fitted with an M33 boom microphone.

Two Seawolves fly across the Delta toward their patrol area. Seawolves operated in pairs to support each other. The assembly above the pilot's head is the weapons sight, swung out of the way.

The shadow of a patrolling Seawolf crosses a Delta village. Sampans are present, but not a single person can be seen, an indicator that there may be VC activity in the immediate area. Even the village is flooded with the houses connected by earth dikes.

While a single M60 machine gun was normally mounted in each side door of a Seawolf, here twin .30-caliber M1919A4 machine guns have been jury-rigged to add firepower.

VNN officers reconnoiter enemy positions over the Mekong Delta aboard a US helicopter. Closest to the camera is a Vietnamese interrupter. The life vests are either bright yellow or international orange.

A PBR Mk II comes alongside a motor junk to inspect its cargo and its crew's identity papers.

A massive Army CH-54 Tarhe, better known as the Sky Crane, cargo helicopter of the 273d Aviation Company (Heavy Helicopter) lifts a PBR Mk II to a new river operating area. The PBR's cockpit canopy was removed and the radar mast stowed for sling operations.

A PACV, its aircraft engine idling, drifts down a river. Even in idle the engine was still loud.

Besides patrolling the river, the considerable canal network had to be patrolled. This view demonstrates the confined nature of canal patrolling and the complete lack of room to maneuver. An ambush at such close range could be devastating.

Constant vigilance was required on river patrols. Detection of even slight movement in riverside vegetation could give the necessary seconds to react effectively.

All sorts of small craft were employed for river patrols. Here a small group of Navy advisors conduct a local patrol in a motorized sampan.

Motorized sampans were rented for such local patrols complete with civilian crewmen.

Regardless of their noise, PACVs were often successful in patrolling due to their high speed. This Dragon Boat intercepts a VC sampan attempting hide to no avail in riverside reeds.

COASTAL PATROL OPERATIONS

Three PCF Swift boats head out to
a to begin their night patrol. The
rn of an LST is to the right.

A division of PCF Swift boats
heads to sea. Once in their patrol area
they would separate to cover specific
sectors, but were still close enough to
provide mutual support.

The routine nature of inspecting
etnamese fishing boats as
monstrated by the .50-calibers
inting skyward, the canvas covered
mm mortar, and unarmed crewmen
nducting the inspection.

`The USS Gallup (PG-85) was the
first Asheville-class patrol gunboat to
arrive in Vietnam (April 1967). The PGs
were assigned to Coastal Squadron 3
operating out of Cam Ranh. This class
of fast gunboat provided heavy fire for
in-shore patrols, it was able to go from
0 to 40 knots in 60 seconds.

On 20 June 1966, the Coast Guard's USCGC Point League (WPB 82304) intercepted and forced aground a North Vietnamese trawler transporting arms to the VC, which burns beyond the cutter's bow. When the cutters arrived in Vietnam waters, they were dressed in Coast Guard white. This proved to be highly visible at night and they were soon repainted gray. In 1969, this cutter was transferred to the VNN and renamed La Van Nga.

A stern view of a PGM patrol motor gunboat. Used by both the US and Vietnamese navies, the PGM was one of the more widely used offshore patrol boats.

The Coastal Surveillance Force could receive fire support from the "Big Gun" or "Blue Water Navy". Seventh Fleet destroyers, destroyer escorts, and light and heavy cruisers patrolled the South China Sea. Here the USS St. Paul (CA-73), a heavy cruiser, steams offshore. Baltimore-class cruisers were armed with nine 8-inch and 12 5-inch guns plus numerous quad 40mm and 20mm cannons.

Destroyers, here the USS Frank E. Evens (DD-754), conducted offshore patrols and escorted cruisers and aircraft carriers. Most classes had a main armament of three dual-mounted 5-inch Mk 12 Mod 1 guns (17,306 yds., 12,200m). The Evans was sunk in 1969 when it collided with a carrier.

The USS St. Paul's forward 8-inch Mk 16 Mod 0 gun turrets could hurl a 250-lb. projectile 31,350 yds (28,000m).

Maritime aerial surveillance was provided by Cam Ranh-based Navy Lockheed P-2H Neptune patrol-bombers. The P-2Hs had white upper-surfaces and light gray under-surfaces as were the stripes on the wings and horizontal tail fins.

A then classified version of the Neptune, the AP-2H attack bomber was operated by Heavy Attack Squadron 21 (VAH-21). It was fitted with low light-level and infra-red televisions to detect targets at night which it attacked with 7.62mm minigun pods and 5-inch Zuni rockets. Its night camouflaging colors were dark, medium, and light grays.

Eighteen Rockwell International OV-10A Bronco observation airplanes, borrowed from the Marine Corps, were used by Light Attack Squadron 4 (VAL-4), the "Black Ponies". Pairs of 7.62mm M60C machine guns were fitted in side sponsons and hard points were provided for 2.75-inch and 5-inch rocket pods and cluster bombs. Navy Broncos were painted either light gray or olive green with white under-surfaces.

A PCF 81mm mortar crew fires on VC positions ashore. The tracer strikes of the .50-caliber machine would be observed to estimate the range and then the mortar fired for effect.

While near inshore, surveillance was constant to safeguard against surprise attacks from VC 57mm and 75mm recoilless rifles ashore. This sailor is armed with a Garand .30-caliber M1 rifle. Some of these were rechambered by the Navy for 7.62mm NATO.

SEALs are best known for their underwater operations using SCUBA ar. Here two SEALs approach an underwater target to emplace a satchel arge carried by the upper man while the lower navigates using a map ard mounting a compass.

When more speed and range was required, the Boston Whaler or Skimmer was used. This one is armed with two M60 machine guns. Another advantage of the Skimmer was its low profile.

In Vietnam the SEALs served ainly as raiders venturing into VC nctuaries to disrupt their movements. Jbber boats were a principal means of ansport in the Mekong Delta's small nding streams. The black rubber ats could be fitted with outboard otors, but silent paddles were the eferred means of propulsion. This uad wears spotted "duck hunter" mouflage uniforms.

A squadron of medium SEAL Support Boats (SSB) depart for a major operation. They are led by a CCB, which will guide them to their release point.

SEALs were also inserted into their areas of operation by repelling from UH-1B helicopters. A SEAL squad could be inserted in this manner in just over a minute.

SEALs patrolling in the Mekong Delta were required to carry necessary water with them as surface water was contaminated. The SEA in the foreground is armed with an M16A1 rifle mounting a 40mm XM1 grenade launcher.

In this sequence of photographs a SEAL patrol surprises a group of VC bold enough to venture forth in daylight. While most SEAL operations took place at night, they also conducted day operations.

The SEALs' boat is a 16-ft. plastic assault boat mounted an M60 machine gun. The boat was actually made of olive drab fiberglass.

Powered by a 40-horsepower Evinrude outboard, the plastic assault boat can be seen to have been camouflaged with palm leafs as it waited in ambush. This group of VC was fortunate in that it was seldom that SEALs did not simply initiate an ambush with overwhelming firepower.

59

From 1968 four-color woodlands camouflage jungle fatigues were issued. A K-bar fighting knife is fastened to his left suspender and a colored smoke grenade, for marking the squad's position to supporting helicopters, is on his right.

Communications with supporting helicopters, boats, and base wa maintained by means of a backpacked AN/PRC-25 or 77 radio. The man i the rear is armed with a 40mm M79 grenade launcher.

This SEAL is armed with an XM16 rifle, the predecessor of the M16A1 The XM16 lacked the bolt forward assist device found on the M16A1. The "bonnie hat" is of the "tiger-stripe" camouflage pattern.

Five of the Navy's 14 Norwegian built Nasty-class fast patrol torpedo boats (PTF) were lost while supporting Special Operations Group 34 (SOG-34 SEAL raids. To replace them severa Osprey-class PTFs were built in the US Powered by two 6,200-horsepowe diesels at up to 40 knots, the aluminum hulled boats were 94 ft. 9 in. (28.8m long with a 23-ft. 2-in. (7m) beam. Thei 14-man crew manned a 40mm cannon two 20mm cannons, and an 81mm mortar. They did not mount torpedoes.

VIETNAMESE NAVY RIVER AND COASTAL OPERATIONS

The French-modified armored Landing Craft, Vehicle or Personnel (LCVP) was commonly used for river patrols. A 20mm Mk 2 cannon was mounted in the bow.

Two .30-caliber M1919A4 machine guns were mounted in the aft side blisters of this armored LCVP. They had limited capability to cover the craft's aft.

A division of four armored LCVPs begin their patrol. Few VNN river craft possessed radar, which limited their ability to interdict VC river traffic.

61

The French-modified armored LCM(6) was the big brother of the armored LCVP. It was used as a troop transport like the US ATC and also provided fire support during river patrol operations.

There were slight variations in the design of LCM(6)s due to differe builders. Note the differences in the bow ramp's design on this LCM wh compared to others.

This monitor does not mount fully enclosed 40mm cannon turr forward as was common, but has 40mm Mk 1 on an open mount with forward shield.

This stern view of an armored LCM(6) displays its three 20mm cannons and two .50-caliber machine guns. Note the tripod-mounted observer's seat or crow's nest.

The French-built STCAN/FOM
[wa]s well-suited for patrolling Mekong
[Del]ta rivers and canals, but it lacked
[spe]ed. Like the armored LCVP, the
["tay-can"]lacked armament capable of
[prot]ecting the boat's stern.

STCAN/FOMs, having been built
in the late 1950s, suffered from
maintenance problems. The engines
were replaced by new American-made
models.

The STCAN/FOM's advantage
[wa]s that it could direct a considerable
[am]ount of firepower in the boat's
[for]ward arc plus was well-protected by
[fro]ntal armor.

Yabuta junk's crewmen were uniformed in either black or gray. Black "pajamas" were common along with black berets, worn here by both VNN crewmen and UN Navy advisors. The advisors wear their US rank insignia on their collars and equivalent VNN rank on their shirt fronts.

This US Navy advisor is armed with a Thompson .45-caliber M? submachine gun and dressed in a black "pajama" uniform. He is esco? by M1 rifle-armed VNN sailors.

A VNN patrol craft crew prepares to inspect a junk. Regular V? sailors wore white sailor caps, light blue chambray shirts, and dark b? denim dungaree trousers, but in practice they tended to dress-do? somewhat.

`VNN Landing Ships, Medi? (LSM) were used for all sorts of coas? transport, logistics support, and ev? fire support. They could transport 4? troops or 250 tons of cargo. The ? Giang (HQ-401, ex-US LSM-90? embarks refugees to be relocated t? more secure area